A Chequered Sea Of Emotions

Kavita Ravindranath

First Published in December 2020

ISBN: 978-93-90030-38-5

BLUEROSE PUBLISHERS

www.bluerosepublishers.com

info@bluerosepublishers.com

+91 8882 898 898

Cover Design:

Kavya Hingorani

Typographic Design:

Namrata Saini

Distributed by: BlueRose, Amazon, Flipkart, Shopclues

About the Author

Kavita Ravindranath was born in the beautiful city of Jamshedpur in 1981.

She did her schooling from D.B.M.S. English School and went to Mumbai for further studies.

Inspired by her experiences in love, friendship and life, she started writing. Appreciated by people around her, she has shared her thoughts through this book.

Currently, she is working in KPS Kadma. She is a teacher by profession and learner by heart.

Acknowledgement

I believe that we all are blessed with the power of feeling our emotions but very few of us are bestowed with the art of expressing them. So, I would like to Thank God for giving me that in abundance.

Being greatly appreciated by my friends — Daljeet Singh, Meghna Singhania, and Ritesh Thakkar, Dipti Parashramka, Richa Verma and many others who always encouraged me to write more — I started believing in myself more because of them.

I won't be able to thank my parents enough for having tremendous faith in me and always being there with me through my struggles.

I thank myself for winning over my own procrastination and for this again I took inspiration from a fabulous book, The Secret of Leadership by Prakash Iyer. Worth reading!

Foreword

Poems or one-liners, romance or philosophy, this collection of thoughts will bring you a waft of freshness of perspective. The words will ring into your ears and occupy your mind long after having been read. They will surely drive you to a different world of random emotions and vibrant notions.

The writer has a mood that is elusive and mercurial — hard to predict the next.

Contents

Inspiration

Uncertainty

Uncertainty makes me feel
In control, natural, spontaneous.
Certainty is fatal, unreal, dubious.
As long as we live, uncertainties keep us company.
When it's time to leave, only death is certain.

Walk your own path

In my morning walks, I look for
The footprints of people who had walked past
Before I did.
I carefully put my feet to exactly fit in.
But before I knew I was trapped in a mess
I hadn't contemplated the result before; yes, I had
thoughtless.
Often in the pursuit of emulating others, we lose our
originality,
We turn a blind eye to all the rationality.
Embrace your shadow, embrace yourself and your footprints.
Carve your own way out,
You sure are allowed to take hints!

Live your moments

Love, hate, wish, do; live life.
Grow, falter, win, lose; live life.
Dance, sing, play, learn; live life.
Smile, cry, yell, pray; live life.
Cos' it's just one life, power pack it!

Chasing peace

When I look at the sea
I see the turmoil at the coast; the horizon deceptively calm.
Life is a journey from the shores to the infinity.
Find beauty in the ripples today; peace is but an illusion.

To the bullies around

I will walk with my head held high,
Keep calling me by whatever name.
Call me a stick, a sack of potatoes, a black crow,
I will not bow down in shame.
I know you are trying to play with me a game,
To bog me down, to dampen my spirits,
But let it be known, your game is pretty lame.
I will rise, and rise beyond all your false claims.
But I wonder what you would have done
If you ever had to go through the same.

Rising in Love

Love means never having to forget who you are.
Never to be disapproved and rejected for what you do.
Never to be asked to step back to let others move ahead.
Never to feel LOW and LONELY at the same time.
Never to be told, you weren't ENOUGH.

From yesterday to today

Cobwebs galore;
Spider ‘yesterday’ at work!
Rip them apart;
Use ‘today’s’ sword.

Happiness

Happiness is often thought to be
Finding reasons to be happy.
Often being expressed as an achievement,
As something acquired or earned.
Often transient, always elusive.
But
Happiness is a state of just being happy.
A smile without a reason,
A splash of mirth in the summer season,
The rise and the fall, the win and the defeat,
The rhythm of the body on the beat.
If it's there it's written on your face in neat,
No faking will get you through the cheat.

The Night

The night is not the time to sleep,
It is for silently creating
The time for the persona to vanish into the darkness,
So the person in you can emerge.
A time to talk to yourself when the world is in deep slumber,
As you awaken to a whole new world within.

Decide what stays

Things that last are often
The things that we want to last.
Anger, greed, discontent, lust,
A broken heart, a want of trust.
If you really don't want them to last,
You've got to work on forgetting them fast.
To leave them behind is a must,
To cling on to them is turning life to dust.

The search of the soul

Looking for the right person is like
Filling in a void.
The bees want nectar, the flowers have it.
The plains need the rivers, the mountains have it.
What do we need? Don't we have it?
Love yourself, pamper as well.
Respect yourself, empower as well.
Your finesse and flaws, celebrate all well.
As you yourself are your heaven and hell.

Diary

New Year resolution

This year
I will not deny myself the right to be happy.
I will not let anyone play me down.
I will not let myself be exploited.
I will not be anything but myself.
#beunputdownable

My Oasis

Far away from here,
There's a world that beckons me
Where I know nobody; where none know me.
Being there, the soul's set free.
Where the sun rises from behind the tree,
Take me to that world where I want to be.

Dear Me

If I could meet you all over again
I would have pampered you with more love,
I would have guarded your respect better,
I would have made you make wiser decisions.
But Dear Me,
I am what I am because of you.
You have shaped me
Through rises and falls, through pain and heal.
How can I ever regret meeting you?

Life

I found life
In the simplest of things.
I found happiness
When I spread my wings.
I found love
When I looked within.
I found purpose
In music and din.

Questions unanswered

I found answers
In no philosophy, no lore.
No hymns, no chants could teach me more.
What lessons can give a sage or a priest?
The verses and books would unravel the least.
Connect to the One who is the creator of all,
And pray for answers from He who made
The universe so vast, the world so small.

If time could speak

If time could speak,
And who said it can't?
It whispered in my ears things that were meant to be,
But I scrapped it as an advice for free.
It warned me loud, it warned me clear,
Of things that I could lose; things that were dear.
Unable to see the unfolding far and near,
Your blurry voices falling on my deaf ears.
In time I have changed, but Time,I guess is still the same.
Hey, Time! I can listen to you crisp and loud,
Talk to me again, I promise you wouldn't have to shout.
In the path of life, I would need you as a friend,
As I am still learning, if I could make amends.

The idea of emotions

When I run out of ideas,
I count on what one never runs out of random emotions.
They keep flowing all the time.
Try tethering them; they ooze, out of proportions.
The genesis of all fiction, faction, narration, relation;
Let go the outburst of emotions.
Sit back and revere the magnificence of the explosions.

Romantic

Wish

I want to spend my evenings with you;
The trivia of the day discussed.
I want to spend my dawns with you;
The hopes for the day focused.
I want to spend the nights with you;
The desire, the love, on our hearts bedecked.
Come, let's spend a lifetime together;
The wish I never expressed.

Heartbeat

Little did I know
The meaning of silence;
The melody of my own breath.
Little did I know
The deep impact of a touch;
The hand to heart undercurrent.
Little did I know
The wonders of a glance;
The heartbeat, the music, the dance.

Love is beckoning

When love arrives, I know not what to do.
If I say 'no' and I let it go,
Do I not deny my heart the right to know,
A man whose touch can make me glow;
A soul that stays with me through high and low?

But if I say 'yes' and usher it in,
I see, I feel, I breathe the magic once again.
It hardly matters whether I lose or gain.
This moment is happy, there is no pain.
So here comes love… it blossoms even in summers!
It sees no time, no place, no reason whatsoever,
It simply flourishes in the hearts of lovers.

A handbook for my lover

i. Love me.
ii. Love me more.
iii. Love me the most.
Simple.

Desire

Drops of sweat rolling down,
The pulse rate high,
Desire running berserk,
The cravings know no bounds,
Give in,
To thy carnal pleasures.

Sarcasm

For the Busy Modern Man (Woman)

Since you have been so busy of late
And couldn't find no time to communicate,
A gentle reminder if you appreciate,
Memories depend on the moments we create.

Without You

It's only without you that
I understood resilience.
I knew the meaning of survival.
You left me stranded
Only to find me on the path of revival.
I'm glad you dumped me;
My success has proved my failure wasn't final.

The Ex Quotient

"I'm in your city."
"Why are you here?"
"They taught us in school, to find X. With time,
the quench has grown."
"Then they must have taught you that X is an
assumption of a value unknown.
I am your X; you knew not my value in times
that have flown.
Now I am priceless; Absolutely knowing
the worth of my own."

www.ingramcontent.com/pod-product-compliance
Ingram Content Group UK Ltd.
Pitfield, Milton Keynes, MK11 3LW, UK
UKHW042001190726
13854UKWH00005B/2101